Essential Music Theory

Answers 5 - 8

Mark Sarnecki

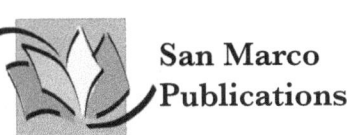
San Marco Publications

Elementary Music Theory © 2023 by San Marco Publications. All rights reserved.

All right reserved. No part of this book may be reproduced in any form or by electronic or mechanical means including Information storage and retrieval systems without permission in writing from the author.

ISNB: 1-896499-42-2

Contents

Level 5:	1
Level 6:	44
Level 7:	78
Level 8:	120

Level 5

Page 2, No. 1

Page 2, No. 2

Page 2, No. 3

Page 2, No. 4

Page 3, No. 5

Page 3, No. 6

Jean Sibelius
Symphony No. 3, III

Page 4, No. 1

G♭	B♭	E#
A#	C♭	F#
D♭	A♭	C#
E♭	B#	G#
F	A#	D#

Page 5, No. 1

3/4	3/4
2/4	2/4
4/4	4/4
3/4	4/4
2/4	3/4

Page 7, No. 1

2/4   2/2   2/4   2/8   2/2   2/8   2/4

Page 9, No. 1

George Frideric Handel
Water Music, X

Joseph Haydn
Symphony No. 92

George Frideric Handel
Concerto Grosso
Op. 6, No. 3

Level 5

Domenico Scarlatti
The Good Humored Ladies Ballet Suite

J.S. Bach
English Suite No. 2

Ludwig van Beethoven
Symphony No. 9, IV

Page 11, No. 1

4/2   4/4   4/2   4/4

Page 12, No. 2

Page 12, No. 3

4/4   4/2   3/2

Level 5

Page 13, No. 1

Page 13, No. 2

Page 14, No. 1

2/4	3/8
4/4	3/2
3/4	2/8

Page 15-16, No. 1

Level 5

Page 17, No. 1

Page 18, No. 2

Page 19, No. 3

Page 20, No. 4

7

Level 5

Page 22, No. 1

Page 23, No. 2

Edvard Grieg
Norwegian Melody

Robert Schumann
Symphony No. 3

Gustav Mahler
Resurrection Symphony No. 1

Level 5

Page 25, No. 1

Page 26, No. 2

3/4
6/8
6/8
3/4

Page 26, No. 3

Page 27, No. 1

Page 28, No. 2

Page 33, No. 1

Page 34, No. 2

Level 5

Page 35, No. 3

Page 36, No. 4

Page 40, No. 1 Review 1

Wolfgang Amadeus Mozart
Piano Concerto K270

Mikhail Glinka
Souvenir of a Night in Madrid

Page 40, No. 2

C#	Db		G#	Ab		F	E#
Ab	G#		B	Cb		Gb	F#
F#	Gb		A#	Bb		Eb	D#
D#	Eb		C	B#		Bb	A#

Page 41, No. 3

Page 41, No. 4

Level 5

Page 42, No. 5

Page 43, No. 6

a) Germany
b) Baroque
c) England
d) A large composition for orchestra, choir and soloists based on a religious theme.
e) 1741
f) Soprano   Alto   Tenor   Bass
g) Technique of writing music that mirrors the meaning of a piece.
h) The text "Forever and ever" is repeated over and over.

Page 44, No. 1

Page 47, No. 1

E natural minor

B harmonic minor

C♯ harmonic minor

C melodic minor

F harmonic minor

A melodic minor

G natural minor

Page 48, No. 2

Page 49, No. 3

19

Level 5

Page 50-51, No. 1

Page 53, No. 1

E♭ major
B♭ major
D minor
G minor
E minor
A♭ major
C minor

Page 55, No. 1

Page 55, No. 2

Page 56, No. 1

Page 56, No. 2

Level 5

Page 56, No. 3

CHS DHS DHS CHS CHS DHS
DHS CHS DHS CHS CHS DHS
CHS DHS DHS CHS DHS DHS
DHS CHS CHS DHS CHS DHS

Page 57, No. 1

Page 57, No. 2

Page 58, No. 1

per 1   maj 2   maj 3   per 4   per 5   maj 6   maj 7   per 8

Page 58, No. 2

per 1   maj 2   maj 3   per 4   per 5   maj 6   maj 7   per 8

Page 59, No. 3

per 1   maj 2   maj 3   per 4   per 5   maj 6   maj 7   per 8

Page 59, No. 4

per 1   maj 2   maj 3   per 4   per 5   maj 6   maj 7   per 8

Page 60, No. 1

Page 60, No. 2

per 8 per 4 min 3 maj 2
per 5 per 4 maj 6 maj 3 min 2

Page 61, No. 3

per 5 min 3 per 4 maj 2 per 8   min 7 maj 7 per 5
per 5 min 6 per 5 min 6 min 7 maj 3 min 7 per 4

Page 61, No. 4

Page 67, No. 1 Review 2

Page 67, No. 2

CHS DHS WS DHS DHS CHS

WS WS WS CHS CHS CHS

Page 68, No. 3

Page 68,

4. An opera is a play with music.
5. Classical era
6. 1791
7. Singspiel
8. German
9. A song in an opera that can be taken out and sung in a musical performance.
10. Coloratura

Page 68, No. 11

b) ***andantino***   a) expressive
a) ***espressivo, espress.***   b) a little faster than andante
d) ***larghetto***   c) very slow
c) ***largo***   d) fairly slow, not as slow as largo

Page 72, No. 1

Page 72, No. 2

Page 73, No. 3

Page 74, No. 1

B♭ C E G D D
F E♭ D E C A

Page 74, No. 2

E	F	G	D	A	A
minor	minor	major	minor	major	minor
2nd inv	1st inv.	root pos.	1st inv.	root pos.	1st inv.

B♭	A♭	B	G	E	F
major	major	minor	minor	minor	major
1st inv.	root pos.	2nd inv.	root pos.	2nd inv.	root pos.

Page 76, No. 1

Page 76, No. 2

Page 77, No. 3

Page 77, No. 4

Level 5

Page 79, No. 1

D major   G major   C major   F major   B♭ major   E♭ major

Page 79, No. 2

Page 79, No. 3

Page 79, No. 4

Page 81, No. 1

Page 82, No. 2

William Byrd
Pavan

J. S. Bach
Toccata and Fugue in G minor

Page 83, No. 3

Dimitri Shostakovich
Symphony No.7, Op. 60

J.S. Bach
Fugue 24 From WTC Book 2

Page 83, No. 4

Frederic Chopin
Sonata in G minor

Claude Debussy
Petite Suite

Level 5

Page 85, No. 1

key: F major

key: C major

key: G major

Page 85, No. 2

key: C major

key: G major

key: F major

Level 5

Page 86, No. 1

Page 88, No. 1

The first phrase ends on: □ a stable scale degree   √ an unstable scale degree

The second phrase ends on: √ a stable scale degree   □ an unstable scale degree

This is a: √ parallel period   □ contrasting period

Page 89, No. 2

key: F major

The first phrase ends on:	☐ a stable scale degree	☑ an unstable scale degree
The second phrase ends on:	☑ a stable scale degree	☐ an unstable scale degree
This is a:	☐ parallel period	☑ contrasting period

Page 90 - 91, No. 1 (other options are possible)

Page 92

1. Who composed the music shown above? **George Frideric Handel**

2. What is the name of the composition? **Messiah - Hallelujah Chorus**

3. What key is it in? **D major**

4. What four voices are used to sing this piece? **soprano alto tenor bass**

5. Name the triad formed by the notes at A **D major triad**

6. Name the interval at B. **per 4**

7. Name the interval at C. **maj 3**

8. Name the interval at D. **per 5**

Level 5

Page 93

1. Who wrote the above musical example? **Wofgang Amadeus Mozart**

2. What musical era was it written? **Classical**

3. What character is singing in this passage? **The Queen of the Night**

4. In what language is she singing? **German**

5. What is the key of this piece? **D minor**

6. Name the triad and inversion at A: **D minor 1st inversion**
   B: **D minor Root position**
   C: **D minor 2nd inversion**

7. Circle one chromatic half step on the score. Label it CHS.

8. Define Allegro assai: **Very fast**

9. How many measures are in this example? **6**

Sonatina

Cornelius Gurlitt
1820 -1901

1. Name the composer of this piece? **Cornelius Gurlitt**

2. Name the key of this piece. **C major**

3. Write the time signature on the score.

4. Define "moderato" **at a moderate tempo or speed**

5. How many phrases are in this example? **2**

6. Does the first phrase end on a stable or unstable degree? **unstable**

7. Does the second phrase end on a stable or unstable degree? **stable**

8. Label the phrases either: (a - a¹⁾) or (a - b) depending on the form.

9. What triad is formed by the notes in the box at letter A: **C major triad**

10. What triad is formed by the notes in the box at letter B: **G major triad**

11. Find the interval of a harmonic minor 3rd, circle it, and label it maj 3.

12. Find the interval of a melodic perfect 5th, circle it, and label it per 5.

13. Find two different diatonic semitones, circle them, and label them DS.

14. How many slurs occur in this piece? **5**

Page 95

Muzio Clementi
1752 -1832

1. Name the composer of this piece? **Muzio Clementi**

2. When did he live? **1752-1832**

3. Write the time signature on the score.

4. Name the key of this piece. **G major**

5. Define "allegro." **fast**

6. Define "dolce." **sweetly**

7. For the triad at letter A, name the: Root **D**   Quality **major**   Position **1st**

8. For the triad at letter B, name the: Root **G**   Quality **major**   Position **root**

9. How many times does the broken tonic triad occur in the bass clef. **4**

10. Find a melodic major 2nd, circle it and label it maj 2.

11. Find a melodic major 3rd, circle it and label it maj 3.

12. Find a diatonic half step, put a box around it and label is DHS.

Level 5

1. Name the key of this piece? **F major**

2. Write the time signature on the score.

3. Check the terms that apply to this time signature. ☑compound ☐triple ☐simple ☑duple

4. Mark the phrases with a slur.

5. Label each phrase using the letters *a*, *a¹* or *b*.

6. Define "andantino." **a little faster than andante**

7. Name the triad at letter A.   root: **F**   quality: **major**

Page 99, No. 1   Review 3

F	G	E♭	D	C	E
major	major	major	minor	major	minor
root	1st	root	2nd	1st	root

A	B♭	A	F	G	C
minor	major	major	minor	major	minor
1st	2nd	root	2nd	root	root

Page 99, No. 2

Page 99, No. 3

c)
d)
a)
b)

Page 100, No. 4

Franz Schubert
Waltz, Op. 50

Page 100, No. 5

Page 100, No. 6

The composer of the Wizard of Oz:
☑Harold Arlen ☐George Gershwin ☐Irving Berlin

Harold Arlen was:
☐French ☐Russian ☑American

"Over the Rainbow" was written for:
☐Bette Davis ☑Judy Garland ☐Beyonce

The song form of "Over the Rainbow" is:
☑AABA ☐ABBA ☐ABAB

Page 105, No. 1 **Exam**

B A G♯ D A

Page 105, No. 2

DHS WS CHS DHS DHS

Page 105, No. 3

Page 106, No. 4

maj 3   maj 7   per 5   min 6   maj 2

Page 106, No. 5

Page 106, No. 6

Page 106, No. 7

W.A. Mozart
Concerto K218

D major

Page 107, No. 8

F major

Page 107, No. 9

i.   ii.   iii.   iv.   v.

Page 107, No. 10

i)
h)
e)
f)
j)
a)
g)
d)
b)
c)

Page 108, No. 11

andantino - a little faster than andante

larghetto - fairly slow, not as slow as largo

rubato - flexible tempo with slight variations of speed to enhance musical expression

largo - very slow

mano destra - right hand

poco - little

lento - slow

pedale - pedal

spiritoso - spirited

marcato - well marked or stressed

prestissimo - as fast as possible

tranquillo - tranquil

dolce - sweetly

leggiero - light

molto - much, very

espressivo - expressive

vivace - lively

fine - the end

marcato - well marked

adagio - slow

Page 109, No. 12

Muzio Clementi
1752-1832

1. What is the key of this piece? **G major**

2. Write the time signature on the score.

3. Define *dolce*   **sweetly**

4. Define *Un poco adagio*   **a little slow**

5. Label the two phrases as: a - a¹ or a - b.

6. For the triad at A, name the: Root: **G**   Quality: **major**   Position: **root**

7. For the triad at B, name the: Root: **D**   Quality: **major**   Position: **1st inversion**

8. Find a chromatic half step in the score. Circle it and label it: CHS.

9. Find and circle a G major scale on the score. Label it: G major.

10. Name the highest note in this piece.   **B**

Level 6

Page 2, No. 1

Page 2, No. 2

Page 3, No. 1

Page 4, No. 2

Jean Sibelius
Symphony No. 3, III

Wolfgang Amadeus Mozart
Piano Concerto K270

Page 6, No. 1

a. Sixteenth note.

b. Eighth note.

c. Half note.

d. Dotted quarter note.

e. Whole note.

f. Quarter note.

Page 6, No. 2

2/4
3/8
2/4
4/4
3/4

Page 7, No. 1

Page 8, No. 1

Page 10, No. 1

Page 11, No. 2

Page 12, No. 3

Page 13, No. 4

Page 15, No. 5

Level 6

Page 16, No. 5

Page 16 - 17, No. 6

12/8
6/8
3/2
9/8
4/2
4/4
6/8
2/4
9/8
12/8

Page 21, No. 1

C#	D	F#	
FCGDAEB	FC	FCGDAE	

G	A	B	E
F	FCG	FCGDA	FCGD

G♭	A♭	C♭	
BEADGC	BEAD	BEADGCF	

B♭	F	E♭	D♭
BE	B	BEA	BEADG

Level 6

Page 22, No. 1

Page 23, No. 2

50 Level 6

Page 24, No. 3 (accidentals are not required descending)

Page 25, No. 4

Page 30, No. 1 **Review 1**

D = E♭♭, Cx

F = E#, G♭♭

F# = G♭, Ex

C = B#, D♭♭

B♭ = A#, C♭♭

Level 6

Page 30, No. 2

or half

Page 31, No. 3

Page 31, No. 4
j)
i)
h)
e)
d)
f)
g)
c)
b)
a)

Level 6

Page 32, No. 5

a. The Baroque period occurred approximately:	☐	1600-1700	☐	1650-1725
	☐	2010-2015	☑	1600-1750
b. The following are famous Baroque composers:	☑	J.S. Bach	☑	Vivaldi
	☐	Mozart	☑	Handel
c. These elements can be used to describe Baroque music:	☑	counterpoint	☑	doctrine of affections
	☐	romantic	☑	highly ornamented
d. These are Bach's 3 main periods.	☑	Leipzig	☑	Weimar
	☐	Berlin	☑	Cöthen
e. Bach composed for the following mediums.	☑	keyboard	☑	orchestra
	☑	choir	☑	chamber music
f. How many 2 part inventions did J.S. Bach write?	☐	21	☑	15
	☐	12	☐	6
g. The 3-part inventions are also known as:	☐	sonatas	☑	sinfonias
	☐	dances	☐	fugues
h. The 2-part inventions are written for this many voices:	☑	2	☐	3
	☐	6	☐	32
i. 3 elements found in the 2-part inventions are:	☑	motives	☑	sequence
	☑	imitation	☐	monophony
j. This is the numbering system used to identify Bach's works:	☐	NRA	☑	BWV
	☐	BVW	☐	BMW

Page 33, No. 1

Page 36, No. 1

E natural minor
B♭ harmonic minor
G♯ harmonic minor
C melodic minor
D♯ harmonic minor
A melodic minor
G natural minor

Page 37, No. 2

Page 38, No. 1

a. The enharmonic tonic major of C♯ major is D♭ major.
b. The enharmonic tonic minor of B♭ major is A♯ minor.
c. The enharmonic tonic major of C♭ major is B major.
d. The parallel minor of D major is D minor.
e. The tonic major of G minor is G major.
f. The enharmonic tonic minor of E♭ major is D♯ minor.

Page 39, No. 2

Page 41, No.1

| per 5 | min 3 | per 4 | maj 2 | per 8 | min 7 | maj 7 | per 5 |
| per 5 | min 6 | per 5 | min 6 | min 7 | maj 3 | min 7 | per 4 |

Page 41, No. 2

Page 42, No. 1

| maj 3 | aug 3 | maj 2 | aug 2 | maj 7 | aug 7 | per 5 | aug 5 |

| per 5 | aug 5 | per 8 | aug 8 | maj 6 | aug 6 | per 4 | aug 4 |

57

Level 6

Page 46, No. 3

Page 47, No. 4

aug 5   min 6   per 5   maj 2   aug 3   aug 4
maj 3   per 8   dim 6   dim 5   dim 2   per 1

Page 47, No. 5

maj 2   dim 4   per 5   per 8   maj 3   min 2   min 3   maj 2

Page 47, No. 6

Page 49, No. 1

per 5   dim 3   maj 6   min 7   aug 2   dim 5

Page 49, No. 2

per 4   aug 5   aug 2   dim 7   dim 7   min 7

Page 49, No. 3

Page 49, No. 4

min 6   min 2   per 4   maj 3
per 4   per 4   min 3   min 3   per 4
per 4   per 4   min 2   maj 2   min 3
maj 2   dim 5   min 2   min 3   per 4

Page 50, No. 1

major   minor   minor   major   minor   major
major   minor   minor   minor   major   major

Page 53, No. 1

B♭   C   E   G   D   D
F   G♭   D   E   C   C♯

Page 53, No. 2

E	F	G	D	A	A
minor	minor	major	minor	major	minor
2nd inv	1st inv	root pos	1st inv	root pos	1st inv

B♭	A♭	B	G	E	F♯
major	major	minor	minor	minor	minor
1st inv	root pos	2nd inv	root pos	2nd inv	root pos

Page 54, No. 1

60

Level 6

Page 55, No. 2

Page 55, No. 3

Page 56, No. 1

C	B♭	E	G	A	E♭
minor	major	major	major	minor	major
root pos	1st inv	root pos	root pos	1st inv	2nd inv

C#	F	B	G♭	E	F#
major	minor	major	major	minor	minor
root pos	root pos	2nd inv	2nd inv	2nd inv	2nd inv

Page 58, No. 1

Page 58, No. 2

| F major | D major | E♭ major | G major | B major | A major |
| F minor | D minor | E♭ minor | G minor | B minor | A minor |

Page 59, No. 1

D major   G major   C major   F major   B♭ major   E♭ major

Page 59, No. 2

Page 59, No. 3

Page 59, No. 4

Page 62-63, No. 1

A major:	A major root pos $\hat{1}$	D major root pos $\hat{4}$	A major root pos $\hat{1}$	
C major:	C major root pos $\hat{1}$	G major 1st inv $\hat{5}$	A minor root pos $\hat{6}$	D minor 1st inv $\hat{2}$
A minor:	A minor root pos $\hat{1}$	E major root pos $\hat{5}$		
G major:	G major root pos $\hat{1}$	D major 1st inv $\hat{5}$		
E minor:	E minor root pos $\hat{1}$	B major root pos $\hat{5}$		

Page 67, No. 1   **Review 2**

Page 68, No. 2

dim 5   dim 5   maj 2

maj 6   min 2   min 7

per 4   per 4   min 3   min 3   maj 3

dim 4   min 2   per 4   min 3

Page 68, No. 3

C	E	B♭	F	A	G
minor	major	dom 7	minor	dom 7	minor
root pos	1st inv	root pos	root pos	root pos	root pos

Page 69, No. 4

k m g i l h c f d j a e b

Page 69, No. 5

a. Who composed Brandenburg Concerto No. 5? **Johann Sebastian Bach**

b. What genre is this work? **concerto grosso**

c. What 3 instruments are featured in this work? **violin, flute, harpsichord**

d. What is this group of instruments called? **concertino**

e. The full string orchestra in a concerto grosso is called a

      ☑ ripieno   ☐ concertino   ☐ oratorio   ☐ sequence

f. The form of the first movement of Brandenburg Concerto No. 5 is

      ☐ rondo   ☑ ritornello   ☐ sonata   ☐ binary

Page 72 - 73, No. 1

	E A			F B♭	
	V I			V I	
A major:	perfect authentic		B♭ major:	imperfect authentic	
	G C			G Cm	
	V I			V i	
C major:	perfect authentic		C minor:	imperfect authentic	
	B E			A Dm	
	V I			V i	
E major:	perfect authentic		D minor:	perfect authentic	
	F B♭m			B Em	
	V i			V i	
B♭ minor:	imperfect authentic		E minor:	perfect authentic	

Level 6

Page 75, No. 1

Page 78, No. 1

Page 79, No. 2

Page 81, No. 1

F major

Page 85, No. 1

Page 88, No. 1

Page 93, No. 1 **Review 3**

F major	F	C
	I	V
	half	

	C	F
	V	I
	perfect authentic	

D major	G	A
	IV	V
	half	

	A	D
	V	I
	perfect authentic	

Page 94, No. 2

G major

Bb major

maj 2

Page 94, No. 3

Page 95, No. 4

9
7
6
8
5
3
2
4
1

Page 95, No. 5

a. T
b. F
c. T
d. F
e. T
f. F
g. T
h. T
i. F
j. T

Page 100

1. Name the key of this piece. **C major**

2. Write the time signature directly on the score.

3. The form of this piece is: ☐ binary ☑ ternary

4. Label the score by using A, A¹, and B to define the form.

5. Define *Allegretto*. **fairly fast, a little slower than allegro**

6. Check all statements below that apply to the chord at A:

   ☑ tonic triad ☐ subdominant triad ☑ C major triad ☑ root position ☐ broken chord

7. Check all statements below that apply to the chord at B:

   ☐ tonic triad ☑ dominant triad ☑ G major triad ☐ 1st inversion ☑ solid or blocked chord

8. Name the cadence at C:

   ☑ perfect authentic cadence ☐ half cadence ☐ imperfect authentic cadence

9. Symbolize the chords of this cadence on the score using functional chord symbols.

Page 101

1. Name the key of this piece. **C major**

2. Write the time signature directly on the score.

3. Check the words below that apply to this time signature.

   ☑triple   ☐compound   ☐duple   ☑simple   ☐quadruple

4. Mark the phrases using a slur.

5. The form of this piece is: ☑binary   ☐ternary

6. Label the score by using A, A¹, and B to define the form.

7. Define *Moderato*. **at a moderate speed or tempo**

8. Name the chord at letter A: **G⁷, the dominant 7th**

9. For the chord at letter B name the: root **C** quality **major** position **2nd inv.**

10. For the chord at letter C name the: root **G** quality **major** position **root pos.**

11. The cadence at D is: ☐half   ☑perfect authentic   ☐imperfect authentic

12. Write the functional chord symbols for this cadence directly on the score.

13. Find and circle a broken dominant triad on the score. Label it DT.

14. Find and circle a broken tonic triad on the score. Label it TT.

Page 102

Joseph Haydn
(1732-1809)
Sonata Hob XVI 34, III

Level 6

1. Name the key of this piece. **E minor**
2. Write the time signature directly on the score.
3. This excerpt is written for a right hand melody with left hand accompaniment. This is and example of:
   ❏ polyphonic music   ☑ homophonic music   ❏ contrapuntal music   ❏ absolute music
4. What musical era was this piece composed? **Classical**
5. Name the chord at A: root **E**   quality **minor**   position **root pos**
6. Name the chord at B: root **B**   quality **major**   position **1st inv**
7. Name the chord at C: root **A**   quality **minor**   position **1st inv.**
8. In this piece, chord A is the: ☑ tonic triad   ❏ subdominant triad   ❏ dominant triad
9. In this piece, chord B is the: ❏ tonic triad   ❏ subdominant triad   ☑ dominant triad
10. In this piece, chord C is the: ❏ tonic triad   ☑ subdominant triad   ❏ dominant triad
11. Define *Molto vivace*: **Very lively**
12. This excerpt is an example of a: ❏ parallel period   ☑ contrasting period
13. Name the interval at D: **min 3**
14. Name the interval at E: **per 4**

Page 109, No. 1 **Final Exam**

dim 5   dim 3   min 6   dim 8   maj 2

Page 109, No. 2

per 4   dim 5   aug 4   maj 6   maj 2

Page 109, No. 3

G major I   IV   V   I

Page 109, No. 4

F major   I   V

I   IV   V   I

Page 110, No. 5

Page 110, No. 6

Muzio Clementi
Sonata for 4 Hands

E♭ major

Muzio Clementi
Sonata for 4 Hands

A major

Muzio Clementi
Sonata for 4 Hands

maj 3

Page 111, No. 7

i.   ii.   iii.   iv.   v.

Page 111, No. 8

Page 112, No. 9

B♭ major   B♭   F
                       I   V
                       half

                       F   B♭
                       V   I
                       perfect authentic

Page 112, No. 10

h   g   d   i   f   c   e   b   a

Level 6

Page 112, No. 11

   a. ***animato***   lively, animated

   b. ***con fuoco***   with fire

   c. ***piu mosso***   more motion, movement

   d. ***senza***   without

   e. ***subito***   suddenly

Page 113

1. What is the key of this piece? **G major**
2. Write the time signature on the score.
3. In what era was this composed? **classical**
4. Define *Allegretto espressivo* **fairly fast and expressive**
5. For the triad at A, name the: Root: **G**   Quality: **major**   Inversion: **root pos**
6. For the triad at B, name the: Root: **E**   Quality: **minor**   Inversion: **root pos**
7. Find a diatonic half step in the score. Circle it and label it: DHS.
8. Find a broken C major triad on the score. Circle it and label it: C major.
9. Name the interval at C. **aug 4**

Level 7

Page 2, No. 1

Page 4, No. 1

Page 7, No. 1

G major
B minor
C minor
E major
F minor
B♭ major
G♯ minor
A minor

Page 8, No. 2

C major
F major
D minor
G♯ minor

Page 10 - 11, No. 1

Joseph Haydn
Quartet, Op. 76

G minor

Joseph Haydn
Symphony No. 99

E♭ major

Johann Sebastian Bach
English Suite 6, Courante

D minor

Frederic Chopin
Nocturne Op. 72. No. 1

E minor

Frederic Chopin
Sonata for Cello and Piano

D minor

Page 13 - 14, No. 1

Page 16, No. 1

Page 17, No. 2

Page 19, No. 1

Page 19, No. 2 (other answers are possible)

Page 21, No. 1 (other answers are possible)

Page 21, No. 2 (other answers are possible)

Page 22, No. 1

Page 23, No. 1

Page 24, No. 1

Page 25, No. 2

84 Level 7

Page 25, No. 3

Page 26, No. 4

A♭ major
B melodic minor
E major pentatonic
C octatonic
D whole tone
F chromatic
D natural minor
A minor pentatonic

Page 32, No. 1 **Review 1**

Page 33

2. When did the Romantic era occur? **1825 - 1900**

3. Music that has a literary or pictorial association is called **program music**

4. Name two Romantic period composers.   **Franz Schubert, Frédéric Chopin, Franz Liszt, Robert Schumann, Johannes Brahms, Felix Mendelssohn, Edvard Grieg, Piotr Ilyich Tchaikovsky, Guisseppe Verdi, Georges Bizet**

5. Where was Felix Mendelssohn born? **Germany**

6. Whose music did Mendelssohn help revive? **J.S. Bach's**

7. What genre is Overture to a Midsummer Nights Dream? **Concert overture**

8. What author wrote the play that this work is based upon? **Shakespeare**

9. What is the form of Overture to a Midsummer Nights Dream? **Sonata form**

10. Name the three main sections in this form. **Exposition, Development, Recapitulation**

Page 33, No. 11

h, d, f, b, g, c, e, a

Page 35, No. 1

aug 5	min 6	per 5	maj 2	aug 3	aug 4
maj 3	per 8	dim 6	dim 5	dim 2	per 1

Page 36, No. 1

Page 38, No. 1

Page 38, No. 2

dim 6   min 3   per 5   dim 4   aug 1   min 7   aug 8   min 6
maj 2   maj 7   maj 3   aug 8   dim 8   min 3   aug 4   min 7

Page 39, No. 3

Page 39, No. 4

maj 2   dim 4   per 5   per 8   maj 3   min 2   min 3   maj 2

Page 40, No. 1

Page 40, No. 2

Page 43, No. 1

2, 3, 3, 3, 6, 7, 7, 7

Page 43, No. 2 and 3

Page 45, No. 1

Page 46, No. 2

12/8, 3/8, 9/4, 3/2, 6/16, 4/2, 6/8

Page 48, No. 1

Page 49 - 50, No. 1

Page 54, No. 1

Page 55

Page 55, No. 2

Robert Schumann
Carnaval (Eusebius)

Franz Liszt
Hungarian Folksong No. 4

Johannes Brahms
Quintet Op. 111, II

Page 57, No. 1

F	E♭m	Ddim	Caug	B♭	Am
G♭aug	F♯m	C	G♯	Adim	D♭aug
Em	Gm	Bdim	D	A♭	Baug

Level 7

Page 57, No. 2

Page 57, No. 3

Page 57, No. 4

augmented   major   diminished   augmented   diminished   minor

Page 59, No. 1

F	C#	A	E♭	D	B
major	minor	diminished	major	augmented	diminished
2nd inv	root pos	1st inv	2nd inv	root pos	1st inv

G	F#	E♭	B	A	D♭
major	minor	minor	major	minor	major
root pos	2nd inv	2nd inv	root pos	1st inv	2nd inv

C	D	C	F#	B♭	E
diminished	minor	major	major	major	minor
root pos	2nd inv	1st inv	root pos	2nd inv	root pos

Page 59, No. 2

Page 60, No. 1

Symbol:	C/E	D♭aug	Am/C	G	Fdim/C	D
Root:	C	D♭	A	G	F	D
Quality:	major	augmented	minor	major	diminished	major
Position:	1st inv	root pos	1st inv	root pos	2nd inv	root pos

Symbol:	Bdim/F	Gm/D	A♭dim	F#/A#	Am	G#aug
Root:	B	G	A♭	F#	E	G#
Quality:	diminished	minor	diminished	major	minor	augmented
Position:	2nd inv	2nd inv	root pos	1st inv	root pos	root pos

Page 62, No. 1

Page 62, No. 2

Page 63, No. 3

Page 70, No. 1

Key:	G minor	A major	B minor	F major
Root/quality:	D^7	E^7	$F\sharp^7$	C^7
Functional:	V^7	V^7	V^7	V^7

Key:	E major	F minor	B major	G major
Root/quality:	B^7	C^7	$F\sharp^7$	D^7
Functional:	V^7	V^7	V^7	V^7

Key:	E♭ major	D major	A minor	B♭ minor
Root/quality:	$B\flat^7$	A^7	E^7	F^7
Functional:	V^7	V^7	V^7	V^7

Page 72, No. 1

Page 72-73, No. 2

A♭	G	F	D	E	D♭
D♭ major	C major	B♭ major	G major	A major	G♭ major
D♭ minor	C minor	B♭ minor	G minor	A minor	G♭ minor
root pos	2nd inv	1st inv	3rd inv	1st inv	2nd inv

F♯	A♭	C	A	G♭	B♭
B major	D♭ major	F major	D major	C♭ major	E♭ major
B minor	D♭ minor	F minor	D minor	C♭ minor	E♭ minor
root pos	1st inv	3rd inv	1st inv	root pos	1st inv

Page 73, No. 3 (other answers are possible)

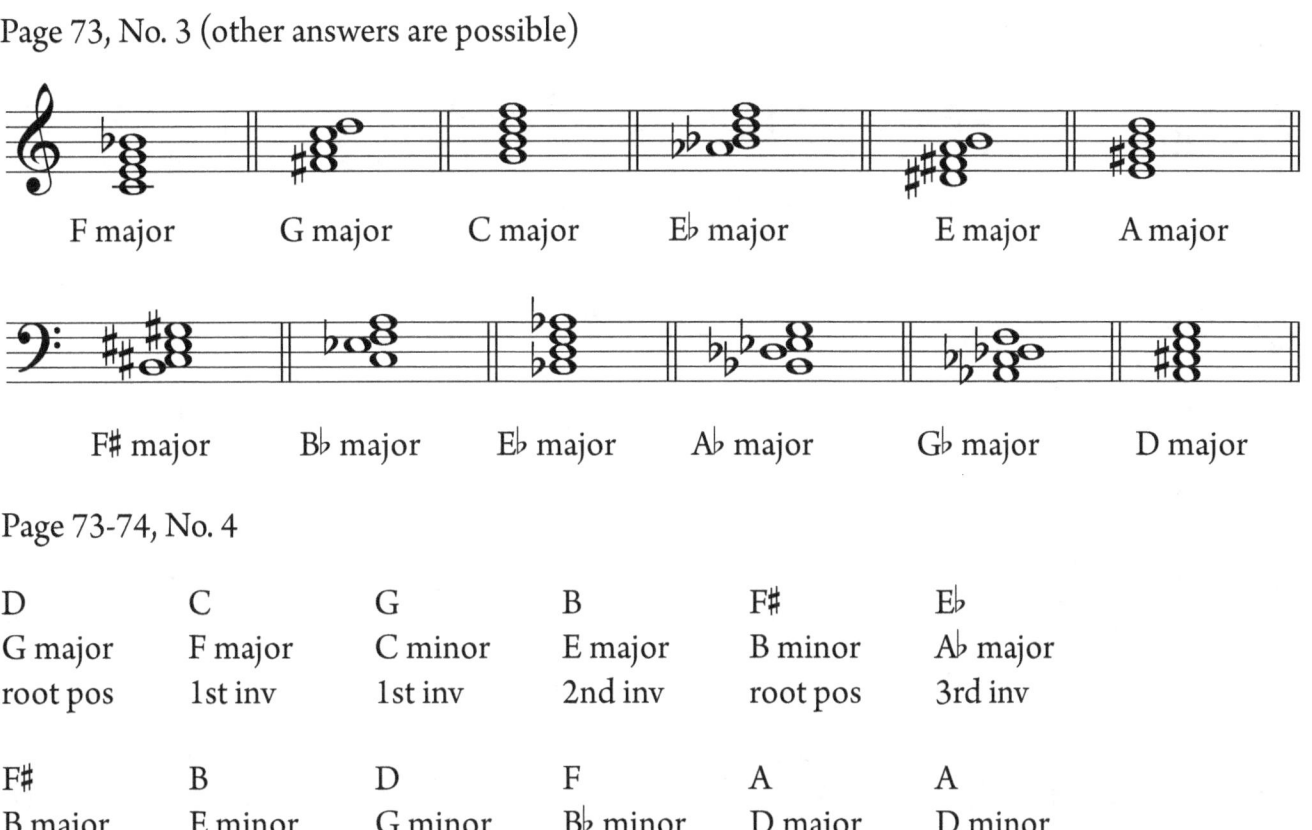

Page 73-74, No. 4

D	C	G	B	F#	E♭
G major	F major	C minor	E major	B minor	A♭ major
root pos	1st inv	1st inv	2nd inv	root pos	3rd inv

F#	B	D	F	A	A
B major	E minor	G minor	B♭ minor	D major	D minor
root pos	2nd inv	2nd inv	root pos	2nd inv	1st inv

Page 75, No. 1

D#dim⁷	F#dim⁷	E#dim⁷	C#dim	Bdim⁷	F*dim⁷
vii°⁷	vii°⁷	vii°⁷	vii°⁷	vii°⁷	vii°⁷
E minor	G minor	F# minor	D minor	C minor	G# minor

Page 75, No. 2

Page 76, No. 1 **Review 2**

Page 76, No. 2

Page 76, No. 3

or a quarter rest

Page 76, No. 4

        martellato   strongly accented or hammered

        morendo   dying away

        pesante   heavy

        scherzando   playful

Level 7

Page 77, No. 5

    V^7 V^6_5 V^7 V^4_2 V^4_3

of A major   of C minor   of D♭ major   of E minor   of F major

Page 77, No. 6

  vii°7   vii°7   vii°7   vii°7   vii°7

of A minor   of D minor   of F minor   of C# minor   of B minor

Page 77, No. 7

F#	G	A	B	G	E
augmented	minor	major	diminished	augmented	diminished
root pos	1st inv	2nd inv	root pos	1st inv	2nd inv

Page 77, No. 8

F, F, T, T, F, F, T, T

Page 81, No. 1

G major:	D G V I perfect authentic	C minor:	Cm G i V half
D minor:	A Dm V i imperfect authentic	A♭ major:	D♭ E♭ IV V half
B minor:	F# Bm V i perfect authentic	A major:	E A V I perfect authentic
A minor:	Am E i V half	D♭ major:	A♭ D♭ V I perfect authentic

Page 85, No. 1 (other answers are possible)

Page 85, No. 2 (other answers are possible)

Page 85, No. 3 (other answers are possible)

Level 7

Page 88, No. 1 (other answers are possible)

Page 89 (other answers are possible)

Page 90, No. 2 (other answers are possible)

Page 92, No. 1

Page 93, No. 2

Page 95, No. 1

Page 96, No. 2

Original key: F major

Page 98, No. 1

Original key: G major

Interval of transposition: per 4

Interval of transposition: maj 3

Interval of transposition: min 6

Interval of transposition: maj 2

Page 100, No. 1

E minor

F major

Page 102, No. 1

A minor

B♭ major

E major

F minor

B minor

Page 103, No. 2 (other answers are possible)

G major

Page 107, No. 1 (other answers are possible)

109

Level 7

Page 117, No. 1 **Review 3** (other answers are possible)

Level 7

Page 118, No. 2

Original key: F minor

Johann Sebastian Bach
WTC Bk. 1. No. 12

C minor

Original key: B minor

Pyotr Tchaikovsky
Symphony No. 6

G minor

Page 118, No. 3

Petrushka
Composer: Igor Stravinsky Genre: Ballet

Koko
Composer: Duke Ellington Genre: 12 bar blues

Dripsody
Composer: Hugh LeCaine Genre: electronic music

Etude Op. 10, No. 12 'Revolutionary'
Composer: Frédéric Chopin   Genre: solo piano piece

Overture to a Midsummer Nights Dream
Composer: Felix Mendelssohn   Genre: concert overture

Page 119, No. 4

f, u, t, v, w, a, b, r, k, s, i, x, l, o, q, p, d, t, j, c

Page 122, No. 1

E minor:	V iv V i	B minor:	iv V i
F major:	I IV V	A minor:	iv V i
D minor:	iv V i	E major:	I IV V I
G♭ major:	I IV V I	G♯ minor:	i V i

Page 122, No. 2

1. tonic   2. dominant   3. subdominant   4. tonic

Page 123, No. 1

A major: I V V
C minor: i V iv

Page 124

1. Felix Mendelssohn
2. Overture to a Midsummer Nights dream
3. Romantic era
4. 8
5. G major
8. per 5, maj 7, maj 6, aug 4
9. very fast

10. sforzando, sudden strong accent
11. perfect authentic
12. Because the piece begins with an incomplete measure or anacrusis.

Level 7

1. Romantic era
2. A♭ major
3. 3/4
4. D♭ major
5. subdominant chord
6. E♭ major
7. dominant chord
8. C: neighbor tones   D: passing tones
9. fairly fast, a little slower than allegro
10. fortepiano, loud than suddenly soft
11. stable

Page 126

George Frideric Handel
(1685 - 1759)

1. George Frideric Handel

2. Messiah

3. Baroque era

4. D minor

5. 3/2

6. simple triple time

7. tonic chord

8. dominant chord

9. subdominant chord

10. 4

11. D: min 3rd   E: min 3rd   F: min 3rd

12. 4

13. 7

Level 7

Page 127

Johannes Brahms
(1833-1897)
Weigenlied Op. 49 No. 4

1. E♭ major

2. 3/4

3. homophonic texture

4. Romantic era

5. Frédéric Chopin, Felix Mendelssohn, Robert Schumann, Pyotr Tchaikovsky, Franz Liszt

7. min 3

8. maj 3

9. dim 5

Page 135, No. 1 **Exam**

G♭ chromatic
D♭ whole tone
C♯ octatonic
E blues
F melodic minor

Page 135, No. 2

Page 136, No. 3

maj 3 aug 3 per 4 dim 5 min 7

min 6 dim 6 per 5 aug 4 maj 2

Page 136, No. 4

G major   half

                                    perfect authentic

Page 136, No. 5

original key: G major

Johannes Brahms
Sextet op. 36

C major

Page 137, No. 6

Page 137, No. 7

d, c, a, e, b

Page 137, No. 8

D minor:	V i	B♭ major:	I V
	perfect authentic		half
C minor:	V i	E major:	IV V
	imperfect authentic		half

Level 7

Page 138, No. 9

a) C major
b) 2/4
c) C   major   root pos.
d) G   dominant 7th   1st inv.
e) C   major   root pos.
f) G   dominant 7th   root pos.
g) E: passing tones   F: neighbor tone
h) min 2
i) anacrusis or pick up
j) humorous, joyful
k) perfect authentic

Page 138, No. 10

Hugh Le Caine	Modern
Frédéric Chopin	Romantic
Duke Ellington	Modern
Felix Mendelssohn	Romantic
Igor Stravinsky	Modern

Level 8

Page 3, No. 1

E A B F G C G F D

E B A E D D C G F

Page 3, No. 2

Page 3, No. 3

Page 4, No. 4

Wolfgang Amadeus Mozart
Cosi fan tutte

Page 4, No. 5

Gabriel Faure
Elegie, Op. 24

Page 8, No. 1

Page 8, No. 2

Page 11, No. 1

Page 12, No. 1

C♮ or C♭ either is correct

Page 13, No. 2

Page 18, No. 1

Page 19, No. 1

F dorian　　　　B♭ mixolydian
G lydian　　　　D aeolian
A locrian　　　　F♯ dorian
E♭ mixolydian　　B lydian
G phrygian

123　　　　　　　　　　　　　　　　　　Level 8

Page 25, No. 1

Page 26, No. 1

Page 27, No. 1

Page 32, No. 1   **Review 1**

Page 33, No. 2

A phrygian
F lydian
E mixolydian
G locrian
C dorian
D lydian

Page 33, No. 3

f, e, d, c, b, a

Page 34, No. 4

G major

B♭ major

Page 34, No. 5

a. F   b. T   c. T   d. T   e. F   f. T   g. T   h. F   i. F   j. F   k. T   l. T   m. T

Page 37, No. 1

Page 38, No. 2

Page 42, No. 1

Page 43, No. 1

Stephen Heller
Op. 119, No. 30

128 Level 8

Pyotr Tchaikovsky
Nutcracker Suite, Danse Arabe

Page 46, No. 1

Page 49, No. 1

Page 50, No. 2

Page 50, No. 3

Page 53, No. 1 (other answers are possible)

Page 57, No. 1

Page 57, No. 2

Page 58, No. 3

Page 58, No. 4

Page 60, No. 1

Page 60, No. 2

Page 61, No. 3

Page 63, No. 1

Page 64, No. 1

Page 64, No. 2

D	A	F#	G	C	D♭
minor	major	dim7	dom7	aug	major
root	1st	root	3rd	root	1st

B	F#	D	C	B♭	E♭
dim7	dim	dom7	minor	major	dim
root	root	root	1st	1st	root

C	C#	G♭	E	F	B♭
dom7	dim7	major	minor	dim	dom7
2nd	root	root	root	1st	1st

Page 65, No. 3

Page 65, No. 4

Page 67, No. 1

e. d. a. h. f. b. c. g.

Page 70, No. 1

Page 71-72, No. 1

		Gm Dm			F B♭
		iv i			V I
D minor:	plagal		B♭ major:	perfect authentic	

		A E			Fm Cm
		IV I			iv i
E major:	plagal		C minor:	plagal	

		Am E			E♭m B♭m
		i V			iv i
A minor:	half		B♭ minor:	plagal	

		A D			Cm G
		V I			i V
D major:	imperfect authentic		C minor:	half	

		E B			Bm C#
		IV I			iv V
B major:	plagal		F# minor:	half	

		F G			D Gm
		IV V			V i
C major:	half		G minor:	perfect authentic	

Page 74, No. 1 (other answers are possible)

137

Level 8

Page 78, No. 1 (other answers are possible)

Page 78, No. 2 (other answers are possible)

Page 80, No. 1 (other answers are possible)

Level 8

Page 81, No. 2

Page 82, No. 3

Page 84, No. 1

Page 87, No. 2 (other answers are possible)

B minor i   V   iv   V

G minor i   iv   i   V

Page 90, No. 1 **Review 2**

maj 10   min 9   per 5   per 12   dim 3   aug 8   min 2   per 11

min 6   maj 7   per 4   per 4   aug 6   dim 8   maj 7   per 5

Page 90, No. 2

Page 90, No. 3

Lili Boulanger
Nocturne

143　　　　　　　　　　　　　Level 8

Page 91, No. 4

Page 91, No. 5

a. the dominant 7th of D major in root position   **A⁷**

b. the supertonic triad of B♭ major in root position   **Cm**

c. the mediant triad of A major in root position   **C♯m**

d. the leading tone triad of F major in 1st inversion   **Edim/G**

e. the diminished 7th of B harmonic minor   **A♯dim⁷**

Page 91, No. 6

sehr	very
mit Ausdruck	with expression
mässig	moderately
langsam	slowly
schnell	fast
bewegt	with movement, agitated

Page 92, No. 7

C minor

E minor

Page 92, No. 8

a, c, a, b, b, c, c, a, c, a, c, a, c, c, b

Page 95, No. 1

F minor

Johann Sebastian Bach
WTC Bk. I, No. 12

A minor

B♭ major

Wolfgang Amadeus Mozart
Divertimento K.229, No. 2

F major

B minor

Pyotr Tchaikowsky
Symphony No. 6

Page 97, No. 1

C major

Allegro

Wolfgang Amadeus Mozart
Clarinet Concerto, K. 622

B♭ major

Page 98, No. 2

E♭ major

Allegro

Johann Nepomuk Hummel
Trumpet Concerto, III

F major

Page 98, No. 3

A minor

Allegretto

Wolfgang Amadeus Mozart
Symphony No. 40, Minuet

G minor

Page 99, No. 1

B♭ major

Allegro

Wolfgang Amadeus Mozart
Concerto for Horn, K.447, III

E♭ major

Page 100, No. 2

G minor

Allegro

Wolfgang Amadeus Mozart
Allegro, K.312

A minor

Level 8

D minor

C# minor

G# minor

D# minor

Page 109, No. 1

Level 8

Page 110, No. 2

Johann Sebastian Bach
Das walt' mein gott

Page 111, No. 3

Ludwig van Beethoven
String Quartet Op 18, No. 1

Level 8

Page 112, No. 4

Franz Joseph Haydn
String Quartet Op 76, No. 3

Page 113, No. 5

Johann Sebastian Bach
O Haupt Voll und Wunden

Page 116, No. 1 (other answers are possible)

Level 8

Page 117, No. 2 (other answers are possible)

B minor   i   iv   i   V

i   iv   V   i

Page 121, No. 1 **Review 3**

B♭ major

Carl Maria von Weber
Clarinet Concerto No.. 1

A♭ major

C major

Wolfgang Amadeus Mozart
Adagio for 2 Horns and Bassoon

F major

F minor

Wolfgang Amadeus Mozart
Concerto for Horn and Orchestra

C minor

Page 122, No. 3

Page 122, No. 4

pizzicato
comodo
stringendo
arco
con sordino
ritenuto

Page 123, No. 5

Page 123, No. 6

a. ***gamelan*** orchestra made up of several types of mallet instruments, or keyboard-style instruments struck with mallets or hammers, as well as different drums, flutes, and occasionally stringed instruments or vocalists.

b. ***metallaphone*** a xylophone-like instrument with metal bars struck by mallets.

c. ***raga*** a mode (scale) found in Indian classical music and used in improvised performances.

d. ***microtone*** smaller intervals than those found in Western music.

e. ***tabla*** a pair of drums that are tuned to work with the notes of the raga.

f. ***tala*** a regular rhythmic cycle found in the raga.

Page 124, No. 1

a. Name the key of this piece. **F major**
b. Write the time signature directly on the score. **6/8**
c. In what musical period was this piece composed? **Classical**
d. Mark the phrases directly on the score.
e. Is this an example of a: ☑ parallel period   ☐ contrasting period
f. Mark the form on the score using the letters **a**, **a¹**, or **b**.
g. State the implied harmony using functional and root/quality chord symbols.
h. Circle and identify any non-chord tones.

Page 125, No. 2

a. Name the key of this piece. **D major**
b. Write the time signature directly on the score. **6/8**
c. In what musical period was this piece composed? **Classical**
d. Mark the phrases directly on the score.
e. Is this an example of a: ☑ parallel period   ☐ contrasting period
f. Mark the form on the score using the letters **a**, **a¹**, or **b**.
g. State the implied harmony using functional and root/quality chord symbols.
h. Circle and identify any non-chord tones.
i. Write the name of the cadences at the end of each phrase in the place provided on the score.

Page 127, No. 1

contrary	oblique	parallel	similar
oblique	parallel	contrary	parallel
similar	oblique	contrary	oblique

Page 128, No. 1

Page 128, No. 2

a. Name the key of this phrase. **B♭ major**
b. Write the time signature directly on the score. **3/4**
c. In what musical period was this piece composed? **Classical**
d. What open score is this written for? **String quartet**
e. State the implied harmony using functional and root/quality chord symbols on the score.
f. Find and circle a melodic sequence.
g. Name the cadence at the end of this phrase. **Imperfect authentic**

Passepied

George Frideric Handel
(1685-1759)

a. Add the correct time signature directly on the music. **3/4**

b. Name the key of this piece. **C major**

c. Name the composer of this piece. **George Frideric Handel**

d. Name another composition by this composer. **Messiah**

d. In what musical era was this composed? **Baroque**

e. This piece is: ☐ monophonic ☑ polyphonic

f. Identify the motion at:

        A: ☐ contrary ☐ parallel ☑ similar ☐ oblique
        B: ☐ contrary ☑ parallel ☐ similar ☐ oblique
        C: ☑ contrary ☐ parallel ☐ similar ☐ oblique
        D: ☑ contrary ☐ parallel ☐ similar ☐ oblique
        E: ☐ contrary ☐ parallel ☑ similar ☐ oblique
        F: ☐ contrary ☐ parallel ☐ similar ☑ oblique

Page 138, No. 1 **Exam**

Page 139, No. 2

maj 10   min 9   per 5   dim 11   aug 12

min 6   maj 7   per 4   aug 5   dim 4

Page 139, No. 3

Page 139, No. 4

Db major

Antonin Dvorak
Scherzo Capriccioso

Gb major

Page 140, No. 5

minor triad   dominant 7th   quartal chord   diminished 7th
polychord   tone cluster   major triad   diminished triad

Page 140, No. 6

Level 8

Page 141, No. 7

Page 141, No. 8

Giovanni Croce
Is it Nothing to You?

Page 142, No. 9

a. ritenuto
b. gamelon
c. con sordino
d. raga
e. Josquin des Prez
f. schnell
g. monophony
h. homorhythmic
i. leger
j. Renaissance
k. Hildegard von Bingen
l. polyphony
m. sitar
n. frottola
o. langsam
p. a capella
q. ostinato
r. Medieval
s. tala
t. plainchant

Level 8

Page 143, No. 10

Lento assai

Ludwig van Beethoven
String Quartet No.16

a) Name the key of this piece. **D flat major**

b) Name the enharmonic tonic minor for this key. **C sharp minor**

c) Write the time signature directly on the score. **6/8**

d) Check two words that describe this time signature:

        ☐simple   ☑duple   ☑compound   ☐triple   ☐quadruple

e) Name the intervals at A: **maj 3**   B: **per 4**   C: **per 4**

f) Define **Lento assai**: **very slow**

g) How are mm.7, 8, and 9 related? **They are part of a melodic sequence**

h) This is an excerpt from a string quartet. What instument is it written for? **violin**

i) Name the four instruments of the string quartet.

        Violin I   Violin II   Viola   Cello

Level 8

www.ingramcontent.com/pod-product-compliance
Lightning Source LLC
Chambersburg PA
CBHW081618100526
44590CB00021B/3491